Your
Dance With God
Faith • Journal

Author and Illustrator
Kathleen L. Rousar

K.L
ROUSAR

Your Dance with God
by Kathleen L. Rousar

First published in 2013 by **Velatura Press LLC**
www.klrousar.com

Unless otherwise stated, all Biblical references are adapted from Young's Literal Translation

ISBN-13: 978-0-9800454-7-5
ISBN-10: 0-9800454-7-9
First Printing, 2013
Printed in the United States of America

This book is the faith journal for *My Dance with God*, also by Kathleen L. Rousar. ISBN: 978-0-9800454-6-8

Velatura Press™ Minneapolis, Minnesota USA

DEDICATION

This journal is dedicated to all of my sisters in Christ. My prayer for us is that viewing these paintings, and then reading God's Word, will increase our capacity to receive God's love. We will then know all the more who we are in Christ, as daughters of the King, in order to be better able to give that love away to others.

Welcome to

Your

Dance With God

Faith • Journal

Introduction

This book, *Your Dance With God*, is a companion to the gift book, *My Dance With God*.

I created this little journal for you to use along side the gift book as you view the Bible verses and images of my artwork.

It will serve as a place for you to write your own prayers and thoughts as you focus on God's Word. You might also use this book as a study guide to share with a group of friends.

Matthew 18:20
Jesus said, "Where two or three join together in My name, I am there with them."

In the first part there are some simple suggestions called:

Questions for Thought

Sometimes we just can't think of what to write. To help, I created 3 easy questions that you can focus on as you read the Bible verses and view the sketches and paintings in the gift book. These questions will help you turn your focus toward the different attributes of God: who He is, how He loves us and how we can share that love with others.

Psalm 26:2-3
Test me Lord, and try me, examine my heart and my mind. Your love is always before me, and I walk continually in your truth.

Next, there are pages for you to write down the prayers you have for yourself and for others:

Pray & Write

Here are spaces for you to date your prayers and to record God's answers. Ask God to lead you to what He wants to reveal to your heart, for yourself and then to minister to others.

The last section of the book is called:

Journal Pages

These are pages for you to write to your Father. You might want to thank God, ask Him something or even question Him. Be sure to keep an open mind and heart. Listen with your spirit to God's still, small voice.

Proverbs 2:6
For the Lord gives wisdom, and from His mouth comes knowledge and understanding.

Have you ever purchased a beautiful journal and been afraid to write in it because you think you might "mess it up?" Or, have you found yourself having a hard time knowing just what to write?

I designed the questions on the following page as suggested guidelines to help you to get started. The questions can help bring each individual verse to life. As you read each verse ask yourself the questions, one at a time, and write your discoveries and thoughts on the blank pages that follow the verses.

Then, in the Journal pages in the back of this book you can write more about how God is personally prompting you to apply the verse to your life.

Assuming that you have the gift book *My Dance With God* to use as a reference, you can also view the drawings and paintings and write about how they minister to you as well.

If you are using the books for a group study you can divide the 22 verses into an 8 week course. The group would go through the verses, 3 per week, ending up with an extra verse for a week of reflection and prayer. Every week, as a group, you can share your insights about the verses. You can pray together, for each other, and for any special needs beyond your group.

Questions for Thought

1. In this verse, how is God . . .

       a. able

       b. good

       c. in control

2. In this verse, how do I see that God . . .

       a. loves ME

       b. created ME

       c. has a plan for ME

3. With this verse, how can I share
   and learn to edify another by . . .

       a. sharing God's love

       b. sharing God's mercy

       c. sharing God's grace

God loves you this way ...

Do you long to experience God's love?

If so, why not settle this right now? Jesus is the evidence that God has a plan for your life. God loves you so much that He gave you the ultimate gift, His son, to pay the ultimate price by laying down His life for your sin. Even if you were the only human being who ever rebelled against God, He loves you so much that He would have sent Jesus to die just for you.

You may have the thought, "No one else has ever loved me this way" – but God does love you this way, and He wants to personally dwell in your heart.

If you are ready to accept Christ, talk to God now, silently or aloud. Tell him, from your heart that you agree with Him when He said that you need a savior, and that Jesus is that savior. Confess that Jesus is the Son of God and that He died for your sins and rose again from the dead. Ask Him to forgive you for your sin and then accept that forgiveness.

God will then become your loving, heavenly Father and you will become His beloved child. The Lord will then give you another gift, the Holy Spirit, who will enable you to experience the free gift of God's love for you.

Begin to read the Bible* by starting with the book of John, in order to learn more about who God can be in your life. John writes about the teachings of Jesus, which reveal the truth of who you are in Him. You will learn that it is only by accepting the truth about yourself that you can become truly free. This is why Jesus proclaimed in John 8:32, "You will know the truth, and the truth will make you free."

*One of the easiest ways, and actually the very best way to obtain a Bible is to call a local Bible-based church. Let them know that you are a new Christian and that you would like to connect and to learn more about following Christ as your personal savior. You could also go to the website called Bible Gateway (www. biblegateway.com), which provides a searchable, online Bible with over 100 versions to choose from.

Job 11:18

And you have trusted because there is hope. You have searched and lie down in safety.

James 4:7

Be subject to God;
stand up against the
devil and he will flee
from you.

Psalm 46:10

Be still, and know that I am God. I am exalted among the nations, I am exalted in the earth.

2 Corinthians 4:18

We are not looking to things that are seen, but to the things not seen; for the things seen are temporary, but the things not seen are forever.

Deuteronomy 30 :10 & 11

Turn towards the Lord your God, with all your heart, and with all your soul. For this command which I am commanding you today is not too wonderful for you, nor is it beyond your reach.

Joshua 23:8

Hold fast to the
Lord your God, as
you have done to
this day.

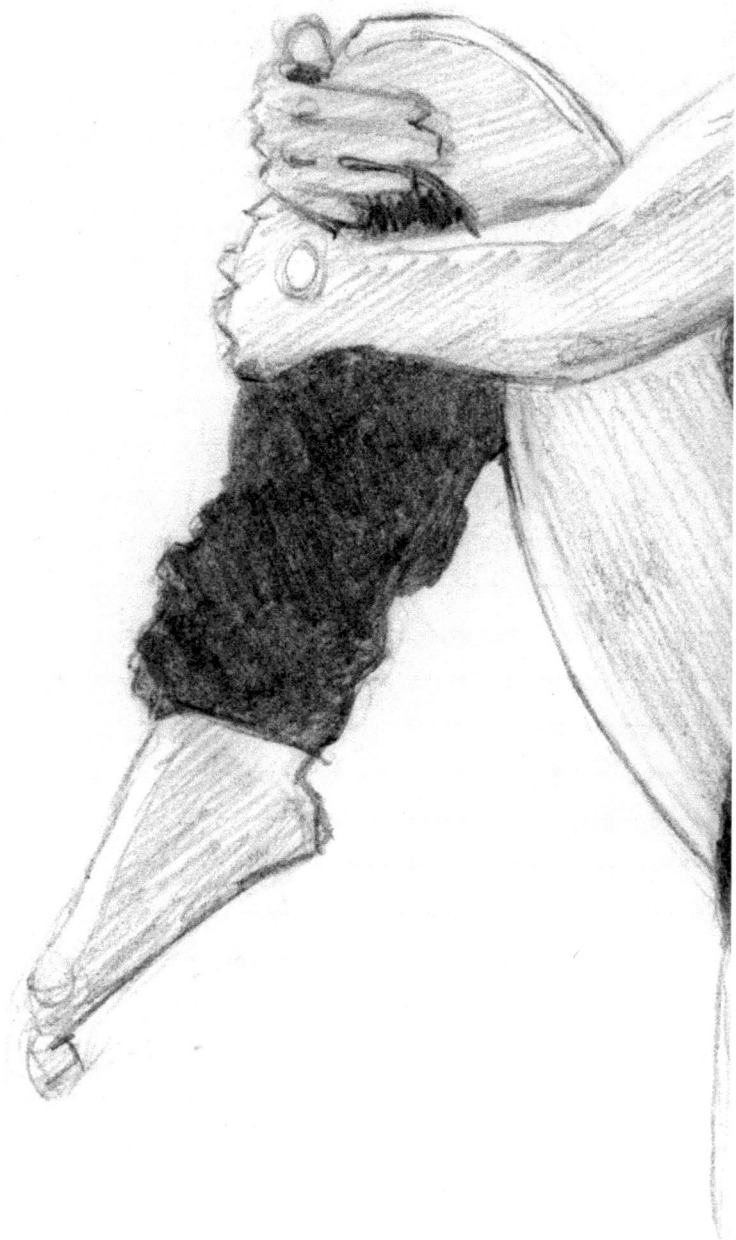

2 Chronicles 20:17

This is not your battle to fight; stand firm, position yourselves, and see the deliverance the Lord will give you.

Psalm 51:10

Create in me a
clean heart, O God,
And renew a right
spirit within me.

Matthew 18:4

Whoever humbles themselves like a child is the greatest in the kingdom of heaven.

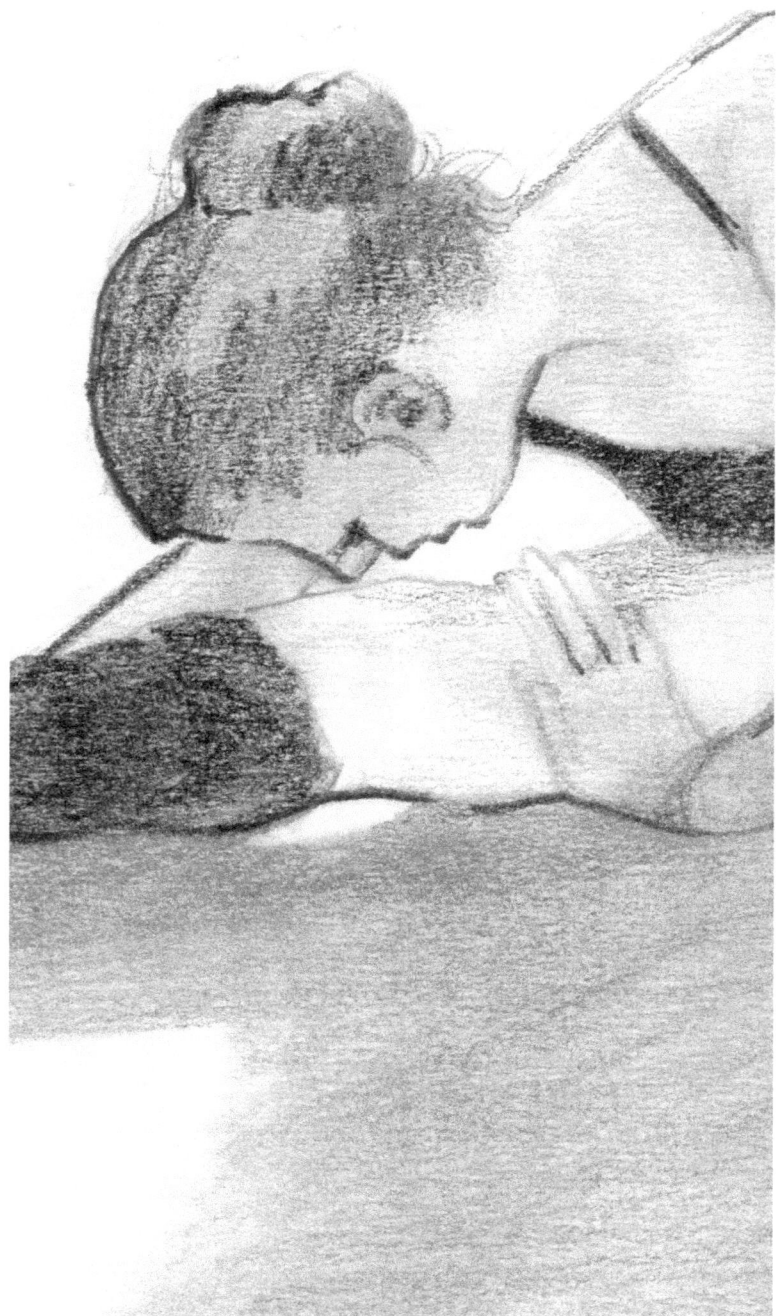

Psalm 31:24

Be strong, and He
will strengthen
your heart, All you
who wait for God!

Psalm 139: 13&14

God You formed me. You formed me in my mother's womb. I will praise You, because I am wonderfully made. Wonderful are Your works, And my soul knows it is well. My substance was not hidden from You when I was made in secret. When I was knit together in the depths of the earth, Your eyes saw my unformed body.

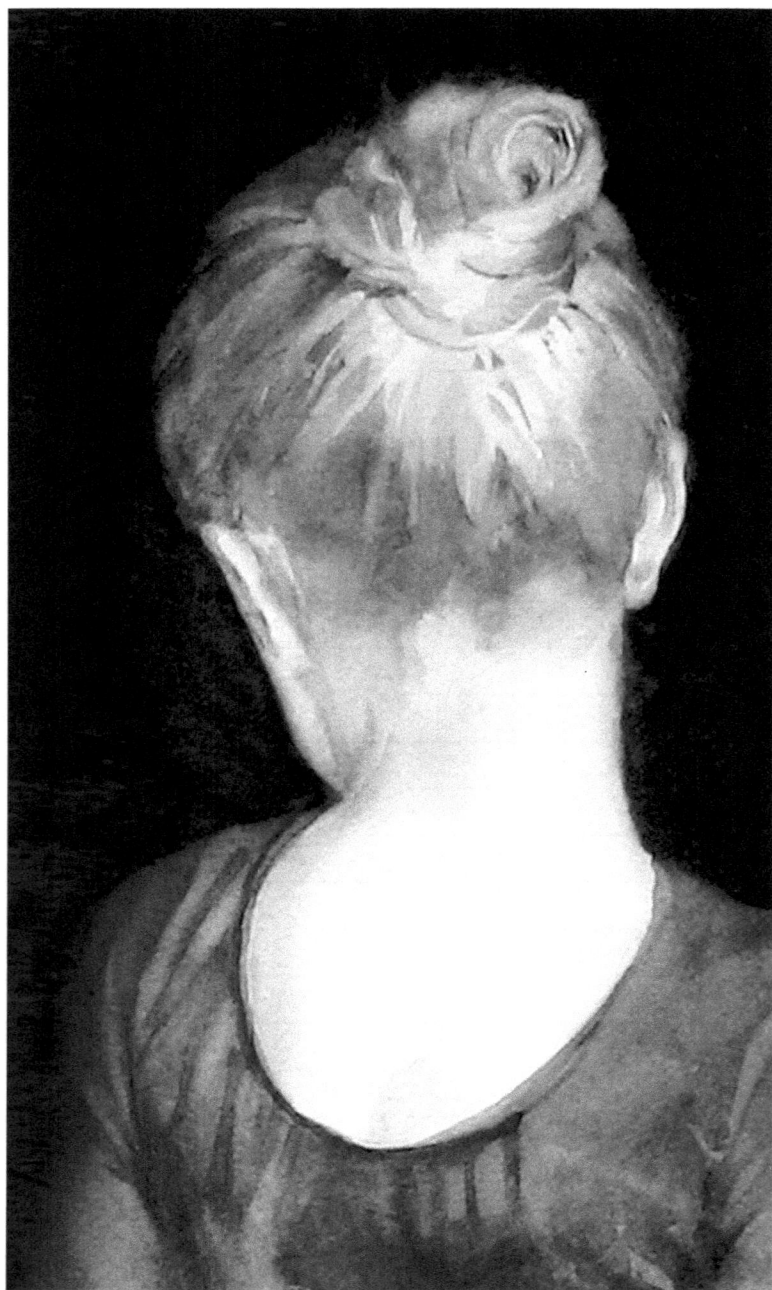

1 John 3:1

How Great the love our
Father has given to us,
that we may be called
children of God; because
of this the world does not
know us, because it did
not know Him.

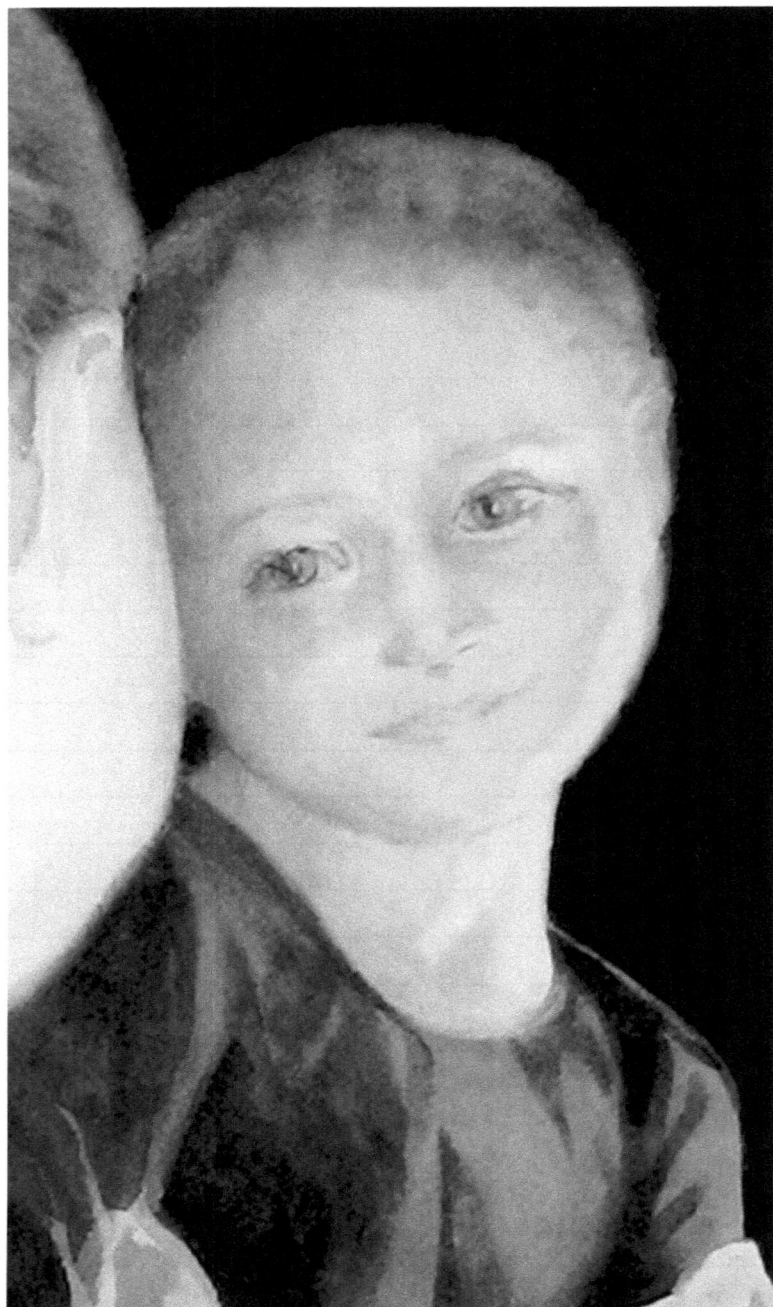

1 Corinthians 13:12

Now we see but a poor reflection in a mirror; then we shall see face to face; now I know in part, and then I shall know fully, even as I am fully known.

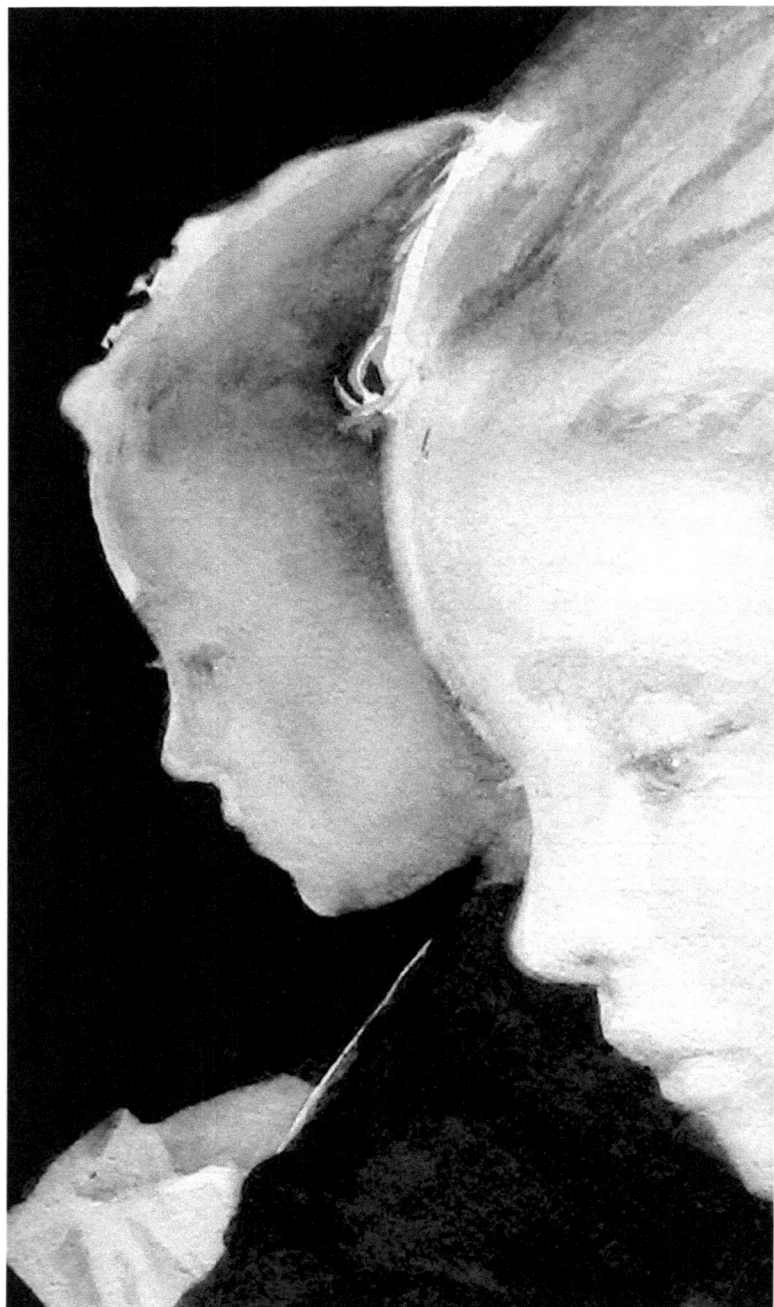

Isaiah 40:31

Those who hope in the
Lord will have their
strength renewed, They
will rise up as eagles.
They run and are not
fatigued. They go on
and do not faint!

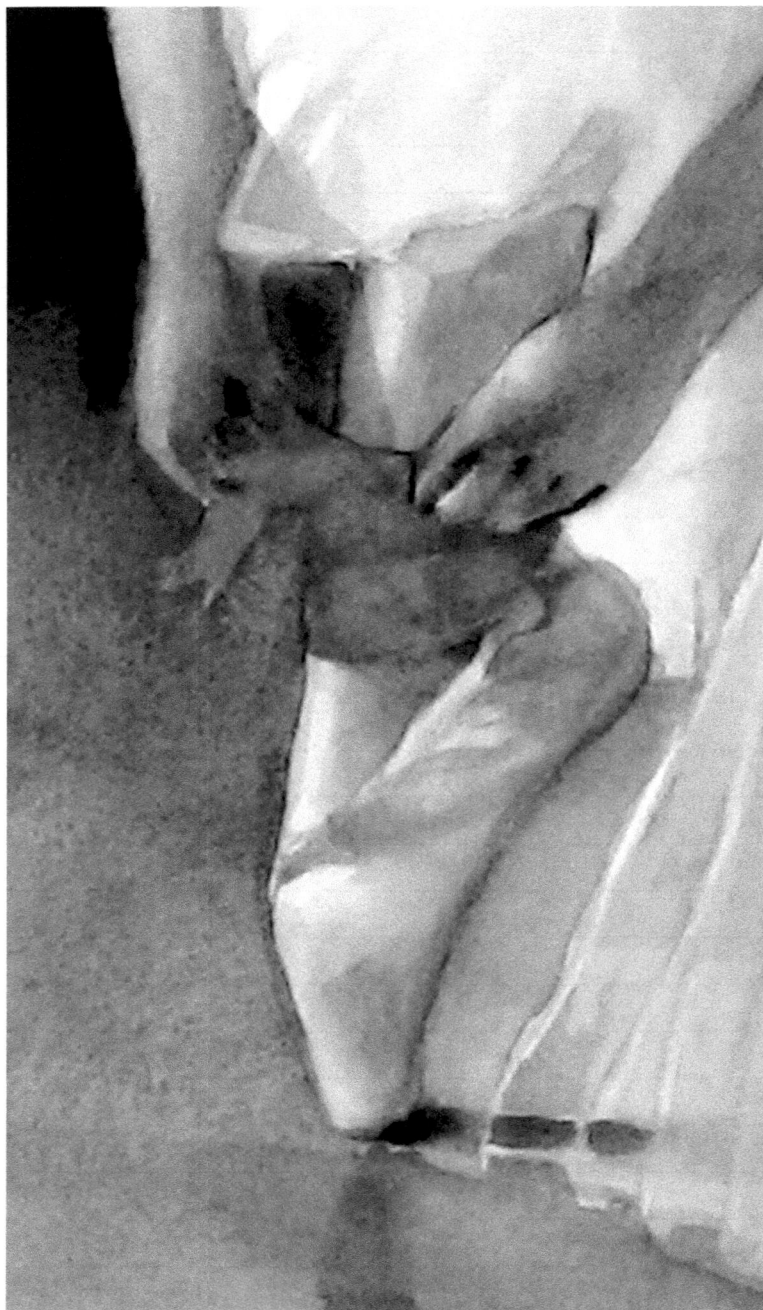

Matthew
11:28-30

Come unto Me, all
who are laboring and
burdened, and I will
give you rest. Take
up my yoke and learn
from Me, because I
am meek and humble
in heart, and you shall
find rest for your souls,
for My yoke is easy, and
My burden is light.

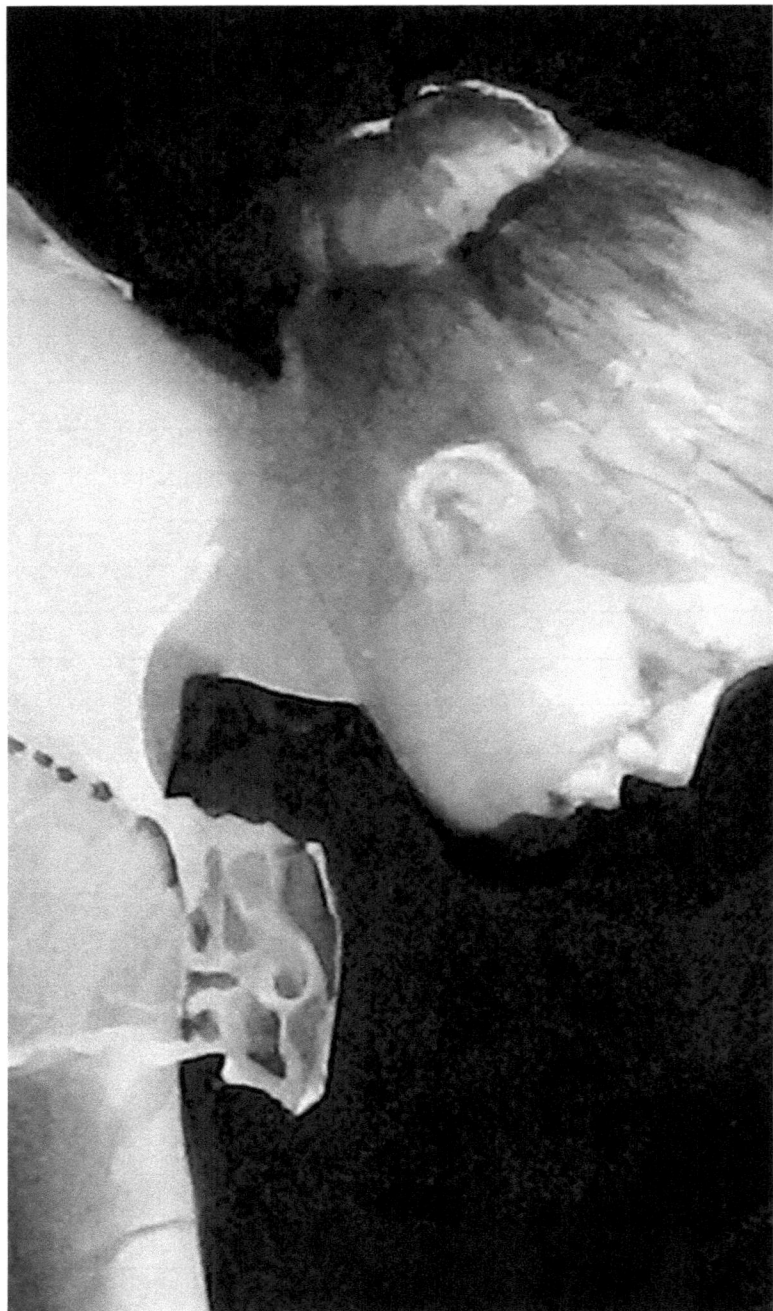

Psalm 51:10-12

Create in me a clean heart, O God, and renew a right spirit within me. Do not cast me away from Your presence, nor take Your Holy Spirit from me. Restore to me the joy of Your salvation, and a give me a willing spirit which will sustain me.

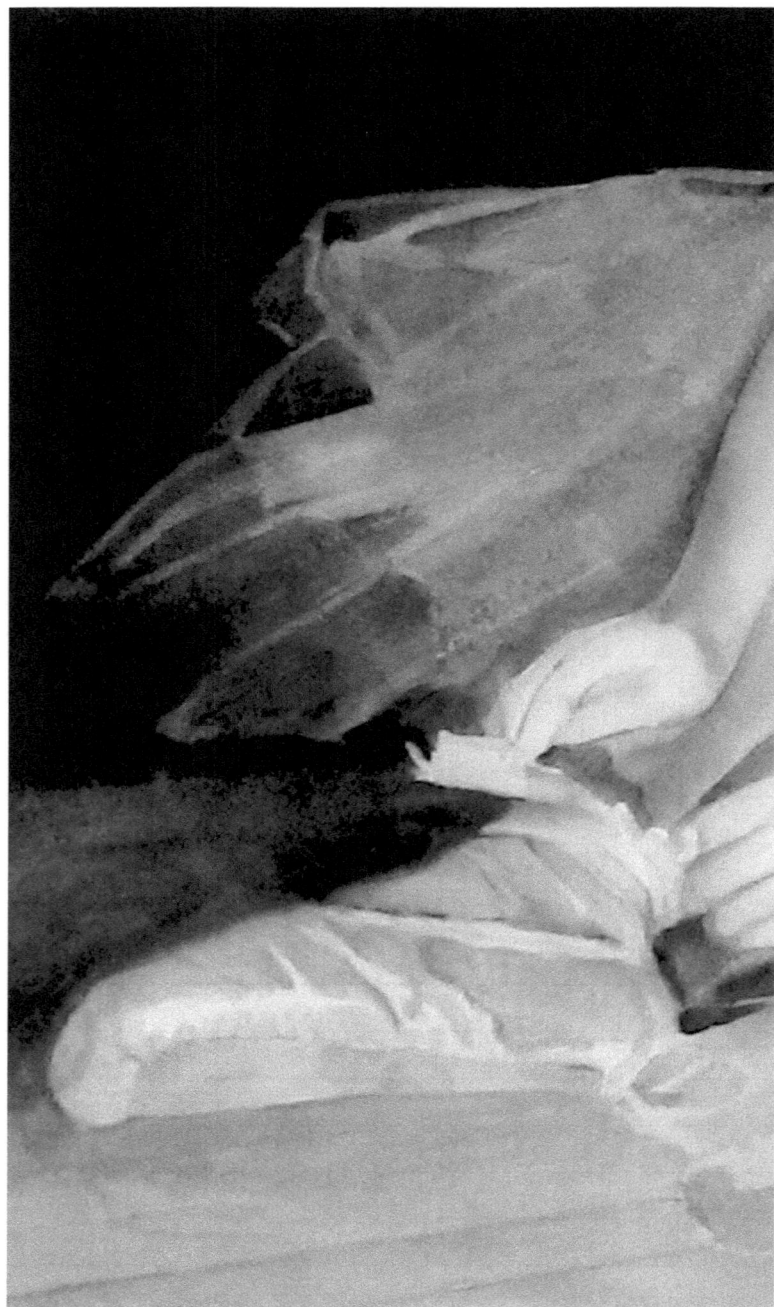

Romans 8:28

We know that to
those who love God
all things do work
together for good, to
those who are called
according to purpose.

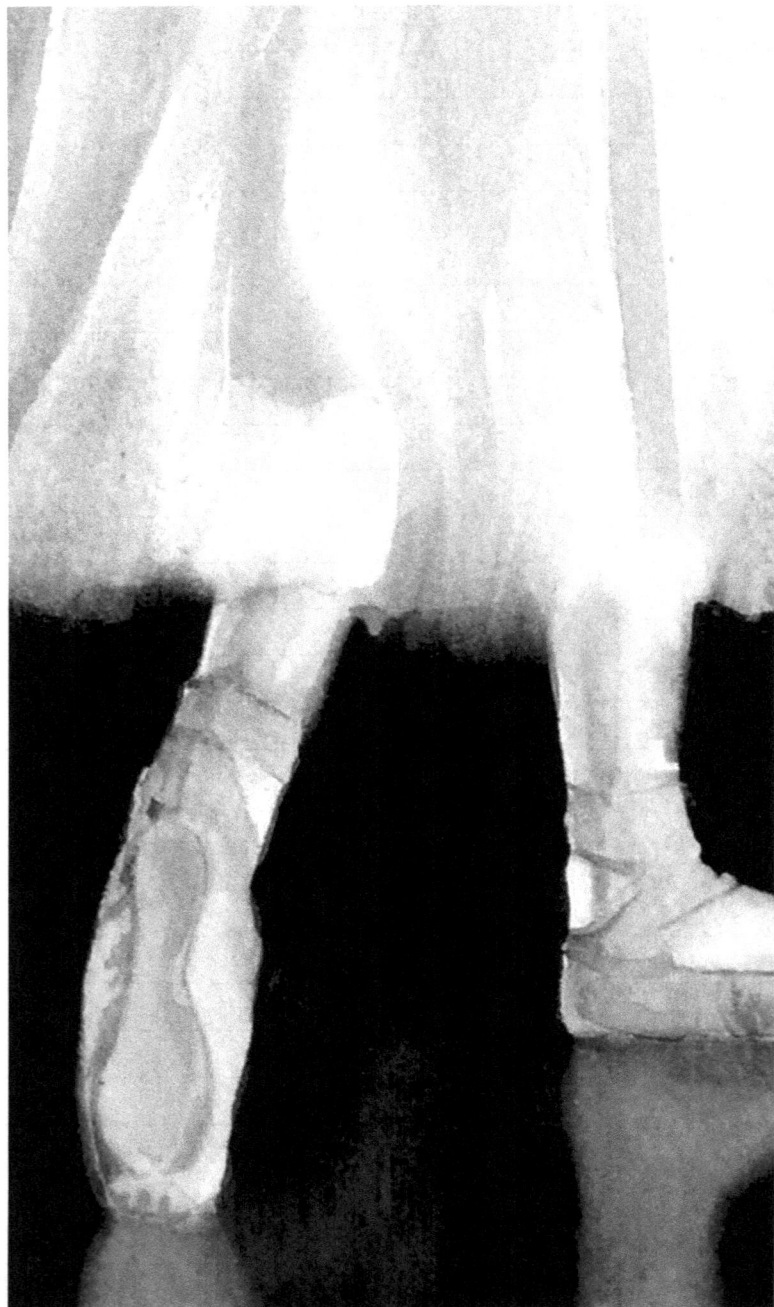

Exodus 15:2

The Lord is my strength and my song, and He is my salvation: This is my God, and I glorify Him; God of my father, and I exalt Him.

Philippians 4:6-7

Be anxious for nothing, but in everything by prayer and supplication, with thanksgiving, let your requests be made known to God; and the peace of God, which surpasses all understanding, shall guard your hearts and your minds in Christ Jesus.

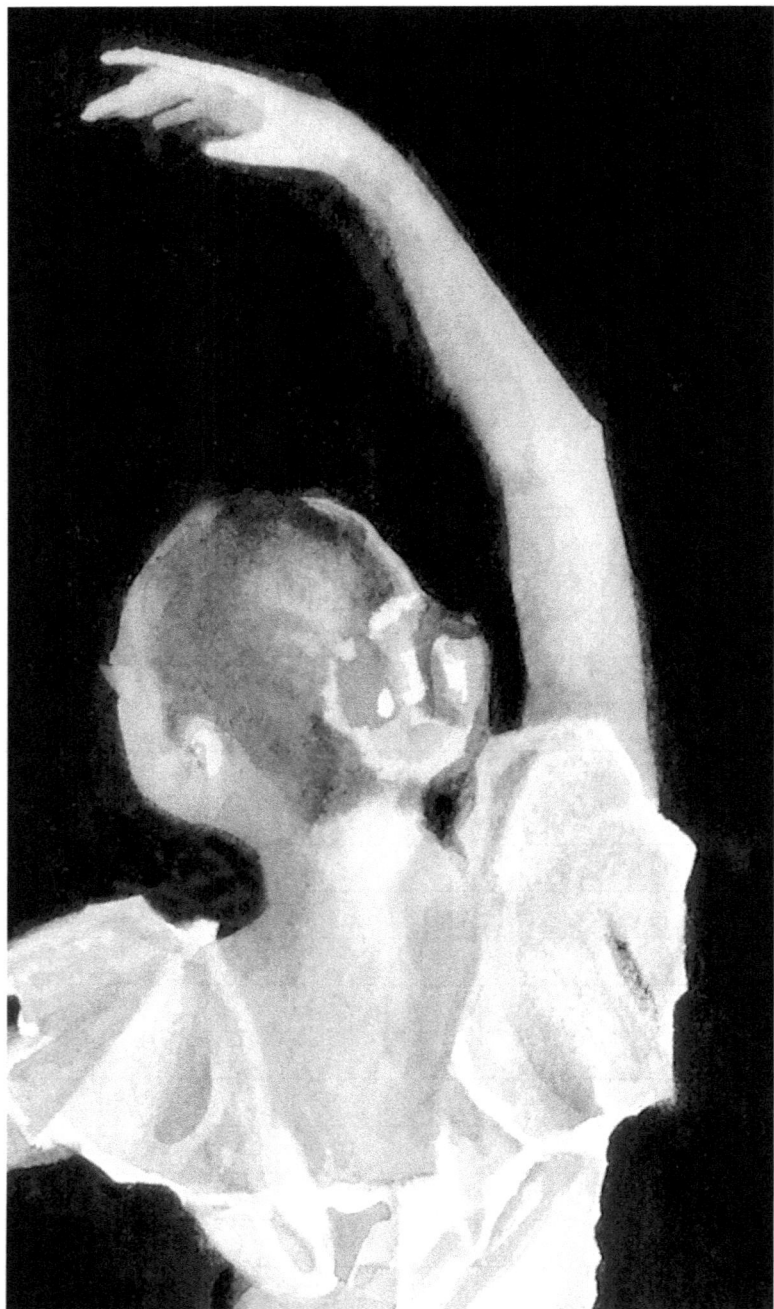

Jeremiah
31:13

Then the young women shall dance and rejoice, both young men and old men together as well. I will turn their mourning to joy, I will give them comfort and turn their sorrow to joy.

Matthew 18:20

'Where there are two or three gathered together, in my name, there am I in the midst of them.'

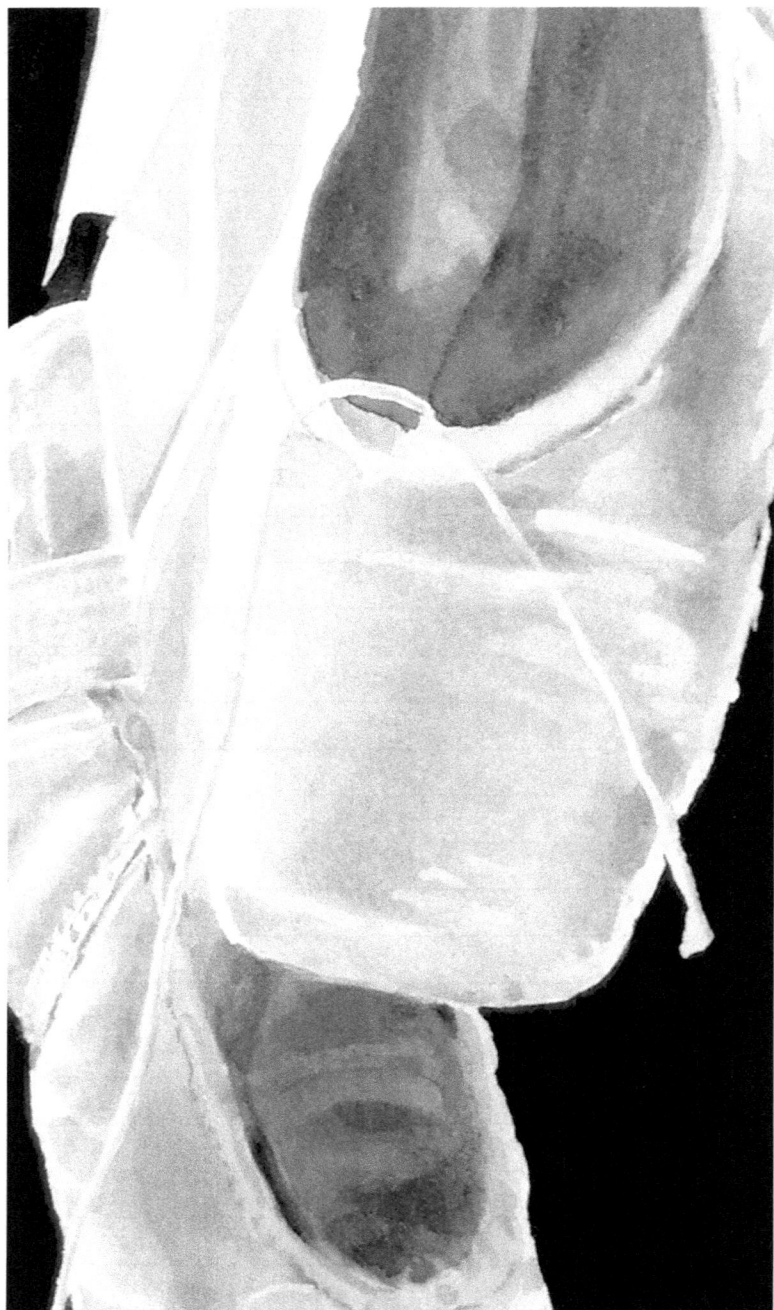

1 Peter 2:21

For to this you were called, because Christ also suffered for you as an example, that you may follow in his steps.

Affirmation

O' Lord, You have searched
me and You know me.
Psalm 139:1

We are God's perfect creation,
created by Him.
God is our Father and
we are His daughters.

*"I am fearfully
and wonderfully made.
I am not a mistake,
even though I make mistakes."*

I praise You because
I am fearfully and
wonderfully made;
Your works are wonderful,
I know that full well.
Psalm 139:14

*"Here I am God
use me!"*

Pray
&
Write

Date:

Name:

Prayer request

Date:

Name:

Prayer request

Date: _____

Name: _____

_____

Prayer request

_____
_____
_____
_____
_____
_____
_____
_____
_____
_____
_____
_____
_____
_____
_____
_____
_____
_____
_____
_____
_____

Date: _____

Name: _____

_____

Prayer request

_____
_____
_____
_____
_____
_____
_____
_____
_____
_____
_____
_____
_____
_____
_____
_____
_____
_____
_____

Date: _____

Name: _____

_____

Prayer request

_____

_____

_____

_____

_____

_____

_____

_____

_____

_____

_____

_____

_____

_____

_____

_____

_____

_____

_____

Date:

Name:

Prayer request

Date: _____

Name: _____

_____

Prayer request

_____
_____
_____
_____
_____
_____
_____
_____
_____
_____
_____
_____
_____
_____
_____
_____
_____
_____
_____
_____

Date:

Name:

Prayer request

Date:

Name:

Prayer request

Date: _____

Name: _____

_____

Prayer request

_____

_____

_____

_____

_____

_____

_____

_____

_____

_____

_____

_____

_____

_____

_____

_____

_____

_____

Date:

Name:

Prayer request

Date:

Name:

Prayer request

Date: _____

Name: _____

_____

Prayer request

_____

_____

_____

_____

_____

_____

_____

_____

_____

_____

_____

_____

_____

_____

_____

_____

_____

_____

Date:

Name:

Prayer request

Date: _____

Name: _____

_____

Prayer request

_____

_____

_____

_____

_____

_____

_____

_____

_____

_____

_____

_____

_____

_____

_____

_____

_____

_____

_____

_____

_____

_____

Date:

Name:

Prayer request

Date: _____

Name: _____

Prayer request

_____
_____
_____
_____
_____
_____
_____
_____
_____
_____
_____
_____
_____
_____
_____
_____
_____
_____
_____

Date:

Name:

Prayer request

Date: _____

Name: _____

_____

Prayer request
_____

_____

_____

_____

_____

_____

_____

_____

_____

_____

_____

_____

_____

_____

_____

_____

_____

_____

_____

_____

_____

_____

Date:

Name:

Prayer request

Date:

Name:

Prayer request

Date:

Name:

Prayer request

Date:

Name:

Prayer request

Date:

Name:

Prayer request

Date: _____

Name: _____

_____

Prayer request

_____

_____

_____

_____

_____

_____

_____

_____

_____

_____

_____

_____

_____

_____

_____

_____

_____

_____

_____

_____

_____

Date: _____

Name: _____

_____

Prayer request
_____

_____

_____

_____

_____

_____

_____

_____

_____

_____

_____

_____

_____

_____

_____

_____

_____

_____

_____

_____

My
Journal
Pages

About me . . .

I have always been creative and intensely interested in expressing myself through painting and drawing. I am in my mid-fifties and am primarily self taught. I began painting full-time a few years ago and I work primarily in watercolor. My reference material comes from life, my imagination and my original photographs. I currently devote my days to painting and intercessory prayer. A few years ago I also began writing and I now keep three daily painting and writing journals. Because I am a Christian I have dedicated my life's work to the glory of God and I want to share the beauty that I see in God's world through my artwork and writing. I am convinced that no matter who you are, how old you are, or what resources you possess, you can discover your own unique, God-given creative ability. I want to share this hope by encouraging you to discover who you are uniquely created to be in Christ. In the future I look forward to getting back to teaching workshops and will continue painting and writing as God leads.

As I share with you a bit of my journey as a Christian, I pray that you will identify with my struggle and find a new hope, as I did, in who God is – your loving Father in Heaven.

I accepted Christ at a young age but even though I have been a Christian for most of my life I have suffered much hardship and I didn't always make the best choices. I never knew my earthly father and the pain of my past left me with a great temptation to blame God for the hurtful actions of others. Through difficult circumstances I lived in the shadows of the wrongs done to me and the guilt over my own mistakes. However, no matter what happened to me in the past the one truth is that God never left me. As long as I sought after Him, He was there. My victory over defeat came when I decided to act on the truth in God's word, that God is greater than any fear, past or present.

These days as I go into my studio to paint, I don't base my actions on where my work will end up or what people may think. I just go and do my task for the day. I start my day praising God and I no longer wait to feel good to act. Instead, I act and paint and claim that God is with me no matter how my painting time goes. This has changed my focus to praising God and I now thank Him for whatever I am able to do that day. As He said in Isaiah 55:8-9, "For my thoughts are not your thoughts, neither are your ways my ways," declares the LORD. "As the heavens are higher than the earth, so are my ways higher than your ways and my thoughts than your thoughts."

When we trust and praise God for who He is, even when we are in the midst of turmoil that we do not understand, our concerns will take on their proper perspective. We can trust that God has a plan, even though we may not see it right now, and know the truth that God is protecting us and working behind the scenes to carry out His perfect plan for our lives.

I once read that before an approaching storm an eagle will seek out a high perch and wait until the first strong winds begin to blow. It then allows those winds to lift it high above the stormy turmoil. I want to encourage you to not give up in whatever storm you may be experiencing right now. You too can rise above your past. You can shift your thoughts from the hopelessness of circumstance and place your hope in the Lord. The storms of life do not have to overcome you. You can rise above the storms that bring disappointment, sickness, tragedy and death upon you by allowing the truth of God's power to lift you up, above them like the eagle. God will enable you to ride out the winds of the storm if you trust and place your hope in who He is.

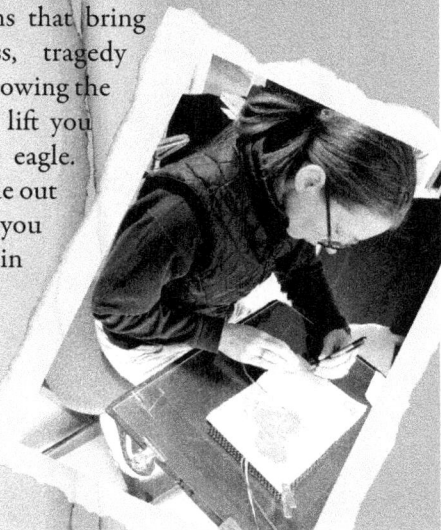

Thank You

-To my husband Darren-
You are the love of my life
and I could have never
done this without your
help and support.

My Prayer for you . . .

-My sisters in Christ-
The Lord bless you
and keep you;
the Lord make His face
shine on you
and be gracious to you;
the Lord turn His
face toward you and
give you peace.
-Amen-

Numbers 6:24-26

To purchase

My Dance With God

www.amazon.com

My Dance with God

A full-color gift book written & illustrated
by Kathleen L. Rousar

Have you ever been desperate for comfort, or felt unable to comfort another in need? *My Dance with God* was born out of just such a need in my life. I hope that this book will serve as a gift to yourself and others, to provide a place of rest for your heart and eyes, through scripture and the images of my artwork.

Jesus is God's greatest gift to us and accepting that gift will change your life. Included in this book is a section called, "*God loves you this way*." If you have not done so already, this is your invitation to accept Jesus as your Savior.

My Dance With God can be read as a devotional, from front to back, or by jumping around. In either case, grab your favorite cup of tea, sit back and relax. I hope that sharing my journey with you will bring you hope and inspire you to allow God to reveal His compassion for you.